HOMEWORK FOR THINKERS

A Year's Worth of Creative Assignments To Stimulate Learning

by Laura Maben

Incentive Publications, Inc.
Nashville, Tennessee

Illustrated by Toni Wall
Cover by Mary Kay Scruggs
Edited by Leslie Britt

ISBN 0-86530-300-2

PRINTED IN THE UNITED STATES OF AMERICA

Table of Contents

PREFACE

Research reveals that effective, high-achieving schools provide meaningful homework assignments on a regular basis. Students learn and retain more when they are asked to apply what they have learned in school to other situations in their lives. The 165 activities in *Homework for Thinkers* are based on these principles.

They were designed to:

- Develop responsibility, independent study habits, and organizational and time management skills
- Provide practice, review, and application of basic skills
- Stimulate creative and critical thinking skills
- Extend classroom learning and encourage lifelong learning

Each activity is based on a high-interest theme which appeals to the elementary student's sense of humor and whimsey and is geared to one of the basic elementary curriculum areas: language arts, mathematics, science, social studies, art, music, health/nutrition, and creative thinking. Grouped thematically, and arranged three activities per page, the teacher will find the pages ready to reproduce and hand out to students as is.

Are First Days Okay?

Write a paragraph about your first day of school this year. Answer these questions in at least five sentences: Who is your teacher? Did you meet any new friends? How did you feel? Did anything good happen? Did anything bad happen?

A School's Name Isn't Plain

Make a list of five new words using the letters in your school's name.

Your School:_____

_____

_____

_____

_____

_____

A Day To Remember

Name a favorite day of the week at school. Write at least six sentences explaining why that particular day is so special to you.

Name _____

Ode To A School

Write a lengthy paragraph explaining why your school is great (use at least six sentences).

Make Time For A Rhyme

Write a word that rhymes with each of the following words:

school _____   write _____

fun _____   books _____

learn _____   me _____

read _____   best _____

Words And Music

Write a song about your school, and give it a title. It may be helpful to use a familiar melody such as Row, Row, Row Your Boat for this song. Once you've written your masterpiece, make an illustration for the upcoming compact disc cover. (Use the back of this sheet if you need more room.)

_____

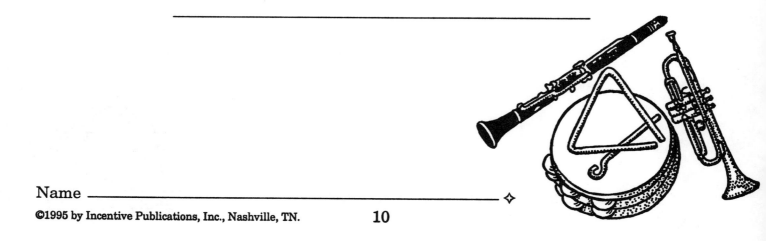

Name _____

Transport Report

On a separate sheet of paper, make a list of all of the different kinds of transportation in your city. Then pick the one that you think is best and explain why in the space below.

Social Studies

Gobs Of Jobs

In alphabetical order, list at least ten different occupations of people in your community.

Science

Clear Or Inclement Sentences

Write at least five sentences describing the climate where you live. Are there ever any extreme weather conditions in your area? Write three more sentences explaining your answer.

Name _____

Important Imports

Prepare a two-column list of items in your home. One column should list items that were made in a foreign country, and the other column should list the country in which those items were made.

Item	Country
Rug	India

Swell Parallels

Find at least five items in or around your house that show parallel lines. List in alphabetical order the items that you find.

Stuffed Full Of Love

In at least five sentences, describe a stuffed animal that is (or was) very special to you.

Name _____

Decorating Descriptions

Write a complete description of your bedroom in at least six sentences.

Social Studies # X Marks The Spot

Draw a detailed map of your bedroom, and include a map legend. Disguise a small X somewhere on the map to show where a secret treasure map is located.

Language Arts # A Room With A Clue

Hide a shoe somewhere in your bedroom. Write specific directions to locate the shoe. Then ask someone in your family to follow your directions.

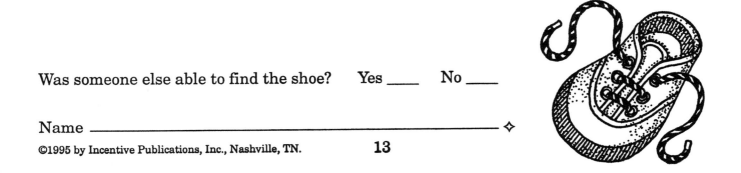

Was someone else able to find the shoe?   Yes _____   No _____

Name _____

Fidget With Digits

Add together all the digits (numbers) in your address. Is the answer odd or even? Now, multiply the answer by 2. Is your answer odd or even?

By-And-By Multiply

Write out the numbers in your telephone number. Then multiply each number by two. What would be your estimation of the total if you added the numbers together? Add all of the numbers to see if your estimation was correct.

Differences In Circumferences

The circumference of an object is the length of the boundary lines in a circle. Measure the circumference of your head, neck, wrist, and ankle using inches or centimeters.

My head: _____

My neck: _____

My wrist: _____

My ankle: _____

Name _____ ◆

Personality Speaking

Create a personality poem by writing your first name in capital letters in a vertical line. Then use each letter of your name to begin a phrase or sentence that tells something about you that is unique.

An example:

Joke books are my favorite.
Outstanding math tests do I take.
Hit home runs,
Never late for school—that's me!

I Dub Thee . . .

Ask your parents (or guardians) to tell you how your name was chosen. Write a **paragraph** that is at least five sentences long describing how you got your name.

Same Name, Same Name

Guess how many times you can write your name in one minute. Put your answer on the following line.

Estimation: _____

Now, actually time yourself. Find a watch that has a sweeping second hand or use an egg timer to see how many times you can actually write your name in one minute.

Name _____

___ # Birthday Banterings ___

Ask a favorite person about their favorite birthday. Write a paragraph of at least five sentences about that special day.

Books Bound To Be The Best ___

Tell about the best book that you've ever read in at least eight sentences. Then draw a picture of the most memorable part. (Use the back of this page, if necessary.)

___ # Playing Favorites ___

In order of preference, make a list of five of your favorite songs. In a short paragraph explain why number one is your favorite.

1._____   4._____

2._____   5._____

3._____

Name _____

"A" Or "An" Articles

Make a list of five words that receive the article "a" and a list of five words that receive the article "an" (example: a trumpet, an orchestra).

A   **An**

_____ _____

_____ _____

_____ _____

_____ _____

_____ _____

Spin Synonyms And Antonyms

Write synonyms (words that have similar meanings) for these words: great, happy, kids, friends, exciting.
Write antonyms (opposite meanings) for these words: happy, dark, easy, boring, sweet.

Synonyms   **Antonyms**

_____ _____

_____ _____

_____ _____

_____ _____

_____ _____

Name An –Onym

Make two lists of synonyms and antonyms.

Synonyms   **Antonyms**

mad—angry   hot—cold

_____ _____

_____ _____

_____ _____

_____ _____

_____ _____

Name _____

Wait 'Til You Hear This!

Write a paragraph of at least six sentences describing the most fantastic day that you have ever had.

Start Clowning Around

If you were a circus clown, what would you do to make people laugh? Explain your answer in at least six sentences.

Many Splendid Things

Food, shelter, water, air, and love are things that people need to live. Why do you believe that love is included in this list? Write at least five sentences explaining your answer.

Name _____ ◆

Appealing Apple Ingredients ————◆

Write your own recipe for a dish that contains apples. Include your list of ingredients and preparation and cooking directions. (Include measurements and time elements.) Then draw a picture of the final product. Use the back of this sheet if you need more room.

◆—— *Language Arts* —— # An Apple Through And Through ——◆

Name ten properties that describe an apple.

1. _____   6. _____

2. _____   7. _____

3. _____   8. _____

4. _____   9. _____

5. _____   10. _____

◆—— *Science* ——— # From Seed To Leaves ————◆

On another sheet of paper, draw a detailed picture of an apple tree (look at a picture from a book if necessary). Label the parts: roots, trunk, branches, leaves, flowers, fruit, seeds. Name the things that a tree needs to live and describe how its seeds are scattered. Be sure to name and date your picture.

Name ——————————————————◆

Somethin' Of A Pumpkin

Estimate the weight and width of your Halloween pumpkin. Guess the number of candies that your family will give out. How many times do you believe that you can say "Peter picked a perfect pumpkin at Pee Wee's pumpkin patch" in one minute? Remember to count the actual answers.

	Estimate	Actual
Weight of pumpkin:	_____	_____
Width of pumpkin:	_____	_____
Number of candies:	_____	_____
Number of times you can say the phrase:	_____	_____

◇ *Mathematics* # A Plucky Pumpkin Problem

Write a pumpkin story problem for the equation $24 \div 6 = 4$.

◇ *Language Arts* # Pumpkin Pulchritude

Describe in at least six sentences the kind of pumpkin that you want to have for Halloween.

Name _____

Halloween Arrangements

Write at least seven new words using a mixture of some of the letters in "Happy Halloween" (example: low).

Creative Thinking/Art

Play It Safe

Halloween is a fun holiday, but sometimes people play a trick instead of getting a treat. Play it safe by making a Halloween poster outlining at least three safety rules that you wish to emphasize. Draw a rough draft of your poster in the space at the right.

Language Arts

Gorgeous Or Grisly Garb?

In at least six sentences thoroughly describe a costume that you have or would like to have this Halloween.

Name _____

Carnival Chronicles ─────✧

Write a classroom carnival list. Include five kinds of game booths, three kinds of food booths, and five prizes for the winners. At the bottom of this list, include the date, time, and location of the carnival.

Games	Food	Prizes
_____	_____	_____
_____	_____	_____
_____	_____	_____
_____		_____
_____		_____

Date: _____ Time: _____ Location: _____

✧ *Art* ───────── # Lines Of All Kinds ─────────✧

Design a poster to advertise your classroom carnival.

Use at least two horizontal lines, two vertical lines, and two diagonal lines on this poster.

Don't forget to include the carnival's time, date, and location on your poster! Draw a rough draft of your poster here.

✧ *Social Studies* ───────── # Mirthful Map ─────────✧

Draw a map of a classroom carnival. Use a map legend to help locate things on your map such as booths and food stands. This can be as elaborate as you would like to make it. (Draw a rough draft of your map in the space below. Draw the final version on the back of this sheet.)

Name _____ ✧

Imagine that you are taking a trip to Disneyland. Estimate the amount of money you should bring for the following necessities.

the entrance ticket _____   dinner _____

lunch _____   souvenirs _____

snacks _____

◇ *Mathematics* ───────── **Try A Surprise** ───────── ◇

If you were to plan a surprise birthday party for your best friend, who would be on the guest list, what games would you play, what refreshments would you serve, and what decorations and party favors would you use? Estimate the total cost of your answer. Total Cost: _____

◇ *Social Studies* ───── **An Ice-Cream Dream** ─────── ◇

If you owned an ice-cream store, what would you name it? What items would you stock? Make a sample menu of all the items that you would sell. On this menu include prices and pictures.

Name _____ ◇

Kindred Spirits

Describe your best friend in at least seven sentences.

Bosom Buddies

List six words that describe what a good friend should be like. Do you have a friend that fits this description? How does he or she fit (or not fit) this description?

Kids' Cool Clubhouse

You are the leader of the Kids Are Cool Clubhouse! Two members, Steven and Brandy, are arguing about whether to paint the clubhouse blue or yellow. The rest of the kids begin to argue, too. The clubhouse needs to be painted before the next week's clubhouse party. How will you solve the dispute? Write at least two solutions and explain why they could work.

Solution One:

Solution Two:

Name _____

Top Ten Thanksgiving Trimmings

Make an alphabetical list of ten of your favorite Thanksgiving foods. Tell which one is your favorite and explain why.

◇ *Creative Thinking* ──── **Finding Foodstuffs** ──────── ◇

Finding Foodstuffs

Think of eight favorite Thanksgiving foodstuffs and use them to design a word-search puzzle.

Example:

T	P	O	M
M	I	L	K
W	E	A	H

◇ *Creative Thinking/Art* **Great Gobblety Goodies** ─────── ◇

Great Gobblety Goodies

Make a menu for the perfect Thanksgiving dinner. Include appetizers to begin the dinner, the main course (with elaborate side dishes), choice of drinks, and dessert(s). Draw a picture of this perfect meal. Use the back of this page if you need more room.

Name ──────────────────────────── ◇

No Place Like Home

List four animal habitats in or near your city. Choose one habitat to describe in detail on a separate sheet of paper.

1. _____   3. _____

2. _____   4. _____

Mathematics

Animal Graphics

Ask ten people to tell you their favorite animal. Make a graph to chart their choices. Which was the most common answer . . . the least common? Who could use this kind of information?

Example:

DOG	√	√	√	√	√	√				
CAT	√	√	√							
BIRD	√	√								
HORSE	√									

Science

Animal Alphabet

List an animal for every letter of the alphabet in the spaces provided below. Choose three animals from the list that you know the least about and research three facts about them. Write your information on the back of this sheet of paper.

A _____   K _____   U _____

B _____   L _____   V _____

C _____   M _____   W _____

D _____   N _____   X _____

E _____   O _____   Y _____

F _____   P _____   Z _____

G _____   Q _____

H _____   R _____

I _____   S _____

J _____   T _____

Name _____

26

A Pet From The Past

Explain in at least six sentences what you think it would be like to have a dinosaur as a pet.

Dinosaur Discoveries

Write three facts and three opinions about dinosaurs.

Facts   1. _____

         2. _____

         3. _____

Opinions   1. _____

         2. _____

         3. _____

Dinosaur Dwellings

Draw a monochromatic (one color) dinosaur in its habitat. Identify its food, shelter, air, and water sources.

Name _____

Dinosaur Lore

Imagine that you have discovered the last living dinosaur. Write at least ten sentences describing what you would do next.

Dividing Dinosaurs

Devise a division story problem for these facts:

    30 dinosaurs are found.

    5 museums want them.

Make sure that you write a story, the equation, and the answer. Use a separate sheet of paper.

Herbivores And Carnivores

Complete a Venn diagram with at least six facts illustrating the differences and similarities between an herbivorous and a carnivorous dinosaur.

Herbivore   Carnivore

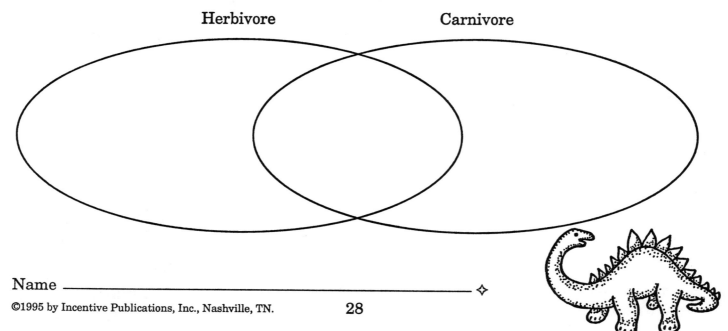

Name _____

Turtle Topics

What would you do if you had a pet turtle? Write a paragraph of at least six sentences answering this question. When you have finished, give your paragraph a "fun" title.

_____
(your title)

Mathematics /
Science

Turtle And Snail Tales

Using a Venn diagram, compare a turtle to a snail. List at least four facts in each section.

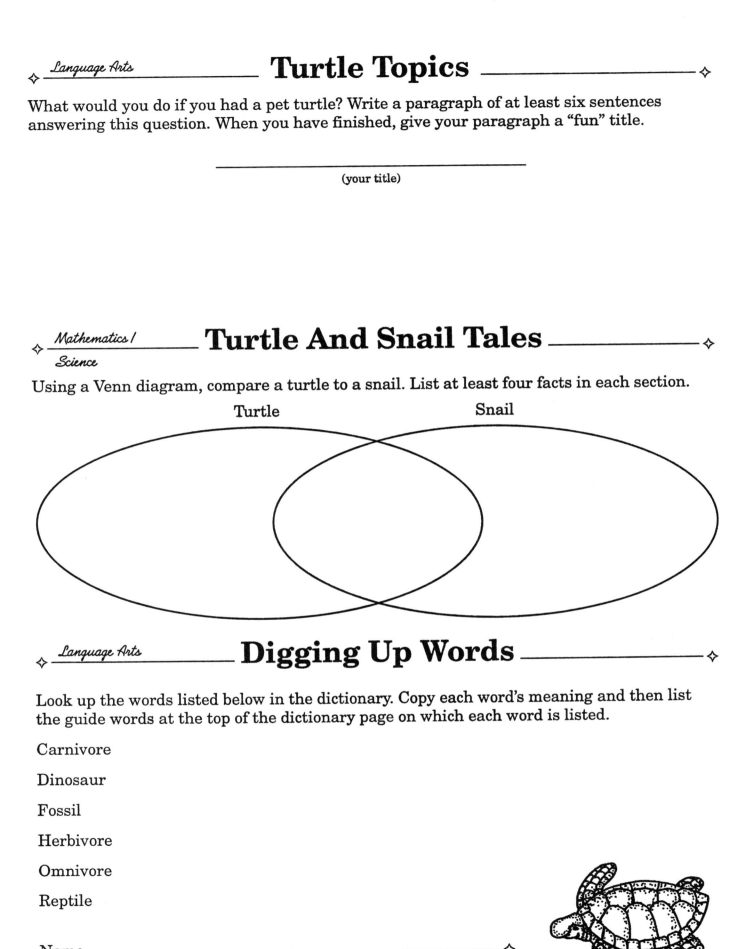

Turtle   Snail

Language Arts

Digging Up Words

Look up the words listed below in the dictionary. Copy each word's meaning and then list the guide words at the top of the dictionary page on which each word is listed.

Carnivore

Dinosaur

Fossil

Herbivore

Omnivore

Reptile

Name _____

Picking Penguins

Color ⅙ of the penguins blue. Color ⅖ of the penguins red. Color the remaining ⅗ any way you choose.

Flying Adventures

Penguins have flipper-like wings, but they can't fly. If you had wings and *could* fly, what adventures would you have? Write at least four sentences telling about one of your adventures.

Bird Bewilderment

Do you think that penguins are really birds? How can you find out? Do some research and write what you discover about penguins in at least four sentences.

Name _____

Swine Sense

Write a multiplication story problem for these facts:
- 5 pig pens
- 7 pigs in each pen

Make sure that you write the story, the equation, and the answer.

Science —— # Mammal Scramble

Is a pig a mammal? Find out the answer and explain how you drew your conclusion using at least three facts about pigs.

Creative Thinking —— # Portly Statements

Here is a funny pig riddle:

What do pigs use when they fall down and scrape their knees?

Answer: Oinkment

Think of two more pig riddles, and write them in the same way in the space below.

Name ————————————

Houndful Happenings

What do you feel would happen if you brought a dog into the school? Write at least six sentences describing one such adventure.

Pooch Ponderings

Do you know the difference between facts and opinions? Write three facts and three opinions about dogs.

Facts
1. _____
2. _____
3. _____

Opinions 1. _____
2. _____
3. _____

Woof Words

Write a paragraph of at least six sentences describing the kind of dog you would like to own. Then draw a picture of your dream dog in the frame.

Name _____

Leonine Or Canine

Use a Venn diagram to graphically compare a cat to a dog. List ways that dogs and cats are both similar and different and write them on the Venn diagram.

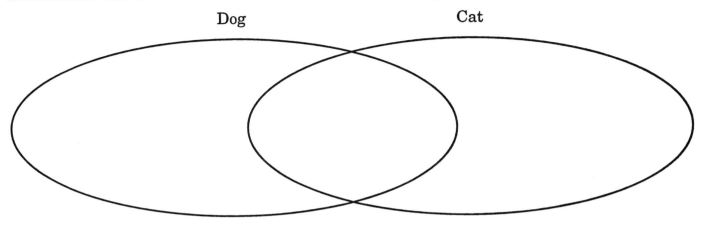

Dog   Cat

Best Pet Yet!

Do you think that a cat or a dog makes a better pet? Explain your answer with three concrete reasons.

That Cat

Fill in the following blanks with adjectives, verbs, and nouns and you will discover that you have written a poem!

CATS

_____cats

_____cats

_____cats

_____cats

All kinds of cats!

A cat that _____ .

A cat that _____ .

A cat in a _____ .

A cat in a _____ .

All kinds of cats!

Name _____

Tool Time ————— ◆

List at least five tools in your house that are not run by electricity.

◆ *Science* ————— # Current News ————— ◆

List at least six machines in your home that are run by electricity.

◆ *Creative Thinking* ——— # Relying On A Robot —————— ◆

Do you think that your life would be different if you had your own personal robot? Explain your answer in at least five sentences.

Name ————————————————— ◆

Moving Words

Write the dictionary definitions of the following words.

automobile:

car:

drive:

engine:

passenger:

What do they all have in common?

Drivers' Education

Design a car safety poster.
Include at least three car safety rules!
Draw a rough draft of your poster in
the space to the right.

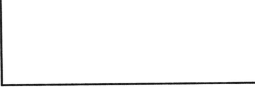

Auto Art

Draw a picture of your favorite kind of car using only primary colors. Then list all of the
geometric shapes that you used in your picture (circle, rectangle, hexagon, etc.).

Name

Invention Mention

Draw a picture of an invention that you wish would be invented but hasn't yet. Explain what it does and how each part functions.

Imagination Goes A Long Way

Find out who Blaise Pascal was and the year he was born. What did he invent and why is that invention significant today?

Can't Live Without . . .

What is your favorite invention? Explain in at least five sentences why it is your favorite. Look up in an encyclopedia, or any other reference book, who invented your favorite invention and in what year he or she was born.

Name _____

Invention Invitation _____ ◇

Invent a machine that your teacher could use in his or her classroom. Draw a picture of it and then name the machine and all its parts.

◇ _Language Arts_ _____ # Have You Heard The News? _____ ◇

Write a newspaper article for the local newspaper telling about your invention. Include a catchy headline and a picture. Write at least three paragraphs for your article. (Use a separate sheet of paper, if necessary.)

◇ _Mathematics_ _____ # Multiplication Explanation _____ ◇

Write a multiplication problem for these facts:
- 7 inventors
- 5 inventions each

Make sure that you write a story, an equation, and the answer.

Name _____ ◇

Creative Thinking — # Ask The Teacher

Write five questions that you would like to ask your teacher. (Make sure that they are questions that your teacher would actually answer.)

1.

2.

3.

4.

5.

Creative Thinking — # Questioning The World

Observe one specific item at home (such as a plant, animal, or machine) for at least ten minutes. Then write five questions that you would like to ask about that object.

1.

2.

3.

4.

5.

Creative Thinking — # Wonder About The Universe

Write eight questions you have about outer space.

1.

2.

3.

4.

5.

6.

7.

8.

Name _____

The Very Idea

Write a well-constructed paragraph (at least six sentences long) describing the best idea that you have ever had.

Growing From Mistakes

Write at least six sentences describing the worst idea you have ever had. Tell in at least two sentences if any good came out of this mistake.

An Illuminating Idea

Who invented the light bulb? Write three sentences to explain who that inventor was **and at** least one more to tell how you arrived at your answer.

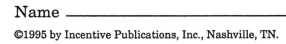

Name

Direct Directions

Draw a map showing the streets that you travel to get from your house to school. Include a map legend and a compass rose (showing the directions of north, south, east, and west).

Social Studies The Contents Of The Continent

Look at a globe or a world map. On it find the seven continents: North America, South America, Antarctica, Africa, Asia, Australia, and Europe. Choose a continent you have never visited, but would like to one day, and write a paragraph telling why you want to go there.

Social Studies Seven Continents And Four Oceans

Draw a map showing the seven continents and four oceans of the world. Label each one.

Name _____

Draw and label the nine planets in our solar system (a mnemonic hint: My Very Eager Mother Just Sat Upon Nine Planets).

Science **A Rising Star**

Does the sun really rise? Explain what happens to the sun in the morning in at least four sentences.

Science **The Daily Planet**

Name five features of the Earth that are different from all of the other planets in our solar system.

Name _____

Sun Illuminations

List six properties of the sun.

1.

2.

3.

4.

5.

6.

Creative Thinking

Sunny Side Up

Make a list of ten activities that you like to do on sunny days. Put the list in order from favorite to least favorite.

1.

2.

3.

4.

5.

6.

7.

8.

9.

10.

Creative Thinking

Sun Glum

Write a paragraph of at least six sentences explaining what life would be like without the sun.

Name _____

Astronaut Or Not?

Would you like to be an astronaut? Write at least three sentences explaining your answer.

Mathematics

Moon Meanderings

Draw a graph with the title "Would You Like To Go To The Moon?" Ask six people this question and mark their responses on your graph. Did more or less people want to go to the moon? Why do you think this is so?

"Would You Like To Go To The Moon?"

YES						
NO						

Creative Thinking

Lunar Luggage

If you were scheduled to leave for a flight to the moon next week, what ten objects (besides clothes) would you pack in your suitcase? Prioritize this list from the most important (number one) to the least important (number ten).

1.

2.

3.

4.

5.

6.

7.

8.

9.

10.

Name _____

◆ Which Watch? ◆

Count the number of clocks in your house (including watches). Then multiply the answer by three. Is the final answer an odd or even number?

Creative Thinking

◆ Party Predicament ◆

Alan's birthday party was scheduled for Saturday at noon at the Cheesy Cheesy Pizza Palace. When Alan and all his friends arrived, the restaurant manager said, "There must be some mistake. Your party isn't supposed to start until 5:00 P.M. The Cheesy Cheesy pizza will not be ready until then!" What do you think Alan should do? Write a list of five helpful solutions to his problem.

1.

2.

3.

4.

5.

Creative Thinking

◆ Morning, Noon, Or Night? ◆

In your opinion, what is the best time of day? Explain your answer in at least three sentences.

Name _____ ◆

Brontosaurus Bewilderment

Amy and Darren both want to research the Brontosaurus dinosaur for their science projects. Their teacher does not want two reports on the same dinosaur. Name two possible solutions to their problem.

1.

2.

Choice Discoveries

If your teacher let you choose any subject for a science project, what would you choose? Write at least three reasons for your answer.

Science Trek

Describe your favorite science project in at least five sentences.

Name _____

A Day For A Sundae

Describe the perfect ice-cream sundae in at least six sentences and then draw a picture of it. What would you call this creative dish? (Use a separate sheet of paper if you need more room.)

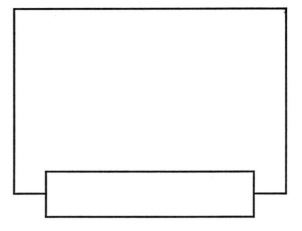

What A Character!

Choose a main character in a book or story that you have read recently and describe him or her in at least five sentences.

The World Around Us

Take a moment to sit in your yard or at the park and experience five minutes of listening. When you have finished, write down where you were and all of the things that you heard, saw, smelled, or felt.

Name _____

Know Your ABABs!

Do some research to find out how the rhyme scheme ABAB works, and then make up a four-line poem which uses that rhyme scheme.

A Maze Craze

Design a maze. (Use a ruler to help you draw straight horizontal and vertical lines.) Mark the beginning and the end points of the maze and ask someone to find his or her way through it.

Teddy's Truth

The teddy bear received its name from one of the United States' former presidents. Discover which president that was and write at least five sentences telling how the bear was named.

Name _____

Nouns Resound

Fill in each of the following categories with at least five more names or items.

PERSON	PLACE	THING
Ms. Maben	California	chalkboard
_____	_____	_____
_____	_____	_____
_____	_____	_____
_____	_____	_____
_____	_____	_____

Language Arts /
Creative Thinking

Puppy Surprise!

What a grand surprise! Your dog has just had six puppies. Make a list of six people that you feel would make good parents to the puppies. Put the list in alphabetical order and explain on a separate sheet of paper why you would give each of these people a puppy.

1.

2.

3.

4.

5.

6.

Creative Thinking

Fact Or Fiction?

Make a list of five of your favorite fiction books or stories. Then make a list of three of your favorite non-fiction books or stories.

Fiction

1. _____
2. _____
3. _____
4. _____
5. _____

Non-fiction

1. _____
2. _____
3. _____

Name _____

A "Hardy" Heart

Trace the symmetrical lines on this heart.

Make another drawing that shows symmetry.
Explain what symmetry is and how it applies to your picture.

Language Arts /
Creative Thinking

Cross Your Heart

Design a word-search puzzle using the following list of words: Valentine, friends, caring, February, red, pink, hearts, cards. Then ask someone to find and circle your words.

Language Arts

Words Of Love

Write a Valentine's card for your teacher. (Use at least four rhyming words in the message.)

Name _____

That Sounds Good

Write a paragraph of at least six sentences describing your favorite song.

Follow The Sound

Make a list of ten places or events where music can be heard (example: a wedding).
In at least five sentences, explain why music is important to you.
(Use the back of this sheet if you need more room to write.)

Two For The Show

Help solve Laura and David's problem. Laura has played the drums for three years.
She is an expert. David has been playing the drums for only a short time, but he has been diligently practicing the drum solo for the school music program. He has not learned it perfectly yet. The music teacher stated that only one person can play the drums for the musical. Who do you believe should play the drums for the school? Give at least three reasons to support your answer.

Name _____

Music Extraordinaire

Write a paragraph of at least six sentences describing the greatest day that you have ever had in your music class at school.

Notes On Instruments

Make a list of ten musical instruments and put them in alphabetical order.

1.   6.

2.   7.

3.   8.

4.   9.

5.   10.

Trumpet Player's Words

Make at least five new words from some of the letters in the phrase "Trumpet Player" (example: tree).

Name _____

Art Smarts

Write a paragraph at least five sentences long describing your favorite art project.

Art/Mathematics

Geometry Is Beautiful

Make an artistic design using the following geometric shapes: five triangles, four trapezoids, three squares, two rectangles, and one hexagon. You may color or paint it when you have finished.

Art/Language Arts

Artistic Endeavors

Who is your favorite artist? Explain in five sentences who this artist is and why you like his or her art work the best. Photocopy or make a drawing of the artist's work, and attach it to this sheet.

Name _____

Taking The Cake

Describe the best birthday party that you have ever attended. (It may or may not be your own!) Make sure that you write at least **six** sentences.

Are You Busy?

If you were going to have a birthday party tomorrow, who would you invite? Put your list in alphabetical order.

Open Invitation

Design an invitation for your own birthday party. Make sure to include the time, date, and location of the party. This is your chance to be creative!

Name _____

Tell Me A Story

Write a creative birthday cake story problem for the equation: 7 x 8 = 56.

A Fraction Of A Slice

Draw a cake that is divided into ten equal parts. Draw chocolate sprinkles on 2/10 of the cake. Draw birthday candles on 3/10 of the cake, and draw a design on 1/10 of the cake. How much of the cake is left plain?

Candle Scramble

Sherri Sugarcane ordered thirteen cupcakes for her brother's surprise party. She was the one who was surprised, however, when fifteen people showed up at the party instead of only thirteen as she had planned. What should Sherri do? Write at least five sentences with suggestions to help her solve her problem.

Name _____

Scoop Scope

Draw a six-scoop ice-cream cone.

Draw chocolate chips on ⅔ of the scoops.

Draw marshmallows on ⅙ of the scoops, and draw nuts on ⅙ of the scoops.

How many scoops will be plain?

Ice-Cream Problem

Write an ice-cream story problem for the equation 7 x 3 = 21.

Deem Your Ice Cream

If you had a $5.00 gift certificate from your local ice-cream store, what items would you buy? How would you budget the money?

Name _____

Ice-Cream Scheme

Make a list of ten of the most popular ice-cream flavors. Then alphabetize the list.

1.   1.
2.   2.
3.   3.
4.   4.
5.   5.
6.   6.
7.   7.
8.   8.
9.   9.
10.   10.

Sweet On Ice Cream

Describe in at least four sentences what is your favorite flavor of ice cream. Then draw a picture of this dessert.

Sweetstuff Solution

Billy and Brenda Sweetstuff are twins. They are going to be celebrating their birthdays on the same day (of course) next week. Billy insists that he wants ice cream, but Brenda wants cookies. Their parents will allow them to have only one sweet treat! What should the twins do to solve their problem? Write at least two possible solutions.

1.

2.

Name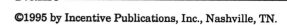

First-Rate Food

Make a list of ten foods that are nutritious. Explain in at least four sentences why you think that these foods are good for you.

1.   6.
2.   7.
3.   8.
4.   9.
5.   10.

Second-Rate Sustenance

Make a list of ten foods that are not good for you. Explain in at least four sentences why you think that these foods are unhealthy.

1.   6.
2.   7.
3.   8.
4.   9.
5.   10.

Foreign Foods

Find three food products in your house that were produced in another country. List the name of each product and the country from which it comes.

Product   **Country**

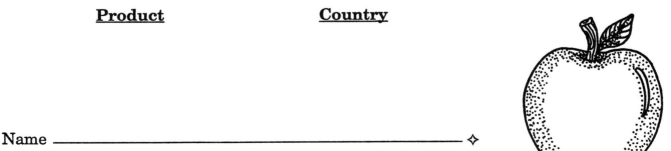

Name _____

Angle Wrangle

How many right angles can you find on this piece of paper? _____

Find at least ten examples of right angles in your home. Name them, and tell where you found each one.

1. _____ _____
2. _____ _____
3. _____ _____
4. _____ _____
5. _____ _____
6. _____ _____
7. _____ _____
8. _____ _____
9. _____ _____
10. _____ _____

Object Objectives

Measure the perimeter of three objects at your house (example: your bed, your room, the garden). Draw a picture of each object and record the perimeter next to each.

Measure By Meter

Make a list of five items in or around your house that measure more than one meter in length and five items that measure less than one meter in length.

Example: **MORE THAN**   **LESS THAN**

door   pillow

Name _____ ◆

Equation Explanation

Write a story problem using the following equation: 346 + 158 = _____. Make sure that you write the story, the equation, and the answer to the problem.

Instrument Inquiry

Write a subtraction or addition story problem which incorporates these facts: 245 pianos, 158 guitars. Write the story, equation, and the answer to the problem.

Flea Market

Write a story problem which incorporates these facts: 226 fleas on Scratchy, the dog; 549 fleas on Itchy, the dog. Write the story, equation, and the answer to the problem.

Name _____

Why, O' Why?

Insert interesting words in the blank spaces and you will find that you have written a poem. (The words don't have to rhyme for it to be a poem.)

I WONDER WHY?

I wonder why _____

I wonder what _____

I wonder how _____

I wonder who _____

I wonder when _____

I wonder if _____

Quite Mysterious!

Write a short mystery story that begins like this, "One fine day at _____ (your school name) in room _____, (your room number) I discovered . . ."

(Continue on the back of this sheet, if necessary.)

Fiddle With A Riddle

Make up three riddles and then write the answers upside-down on the page.

Example: I am furry, friendly, and full of fleas. What am I?

Answer: A dog

Name _____ ✦

A Mickey Mouse Message

Language Arts

Write a convincing letter to your teacher to persuade him or her to allow you to borrow enough money to go to Disneyland. Write at least six sentences.

Dear _____,

Ponder And Persuade

Language Arts

Write a letter to your teacher to persuade him or her to take your class to the beach. Write at least six convincing sentences.

Dear _____,

A Lunar Letter

Language Arts

NASA has sent you to outer space. Write a letter to your teacher describing your experiences (use at least six sentences).

Dear _____,

Name _____ ✧

Vibrant Verse

Create a "color" poem for each of the primary colors (red, yellow, and blue).

RED	YELLOW	BLUE
Red is_____	Yellow is _____	Blue is _____
Red is_____	Yellow is _____	Blue is _____
Red is_____	Yellow is _____	Blue is _____
Red is_____	Yellow is _____	Blue is _____

Turn A Phrase

Write instructions for making the secondary colors of orange, green, and violet. Use the words "first," "second," and "next" to make your instructions clear. You may use crayons, markers, or paint to demonstrate your instructions.

Clowns Of Many Colors

Draw a picture of what you imagine a funny, colorful clown would look like. Then describe him or her in at least five sentences.

Name _____

Sailboat Blueprint

Write easy-to-understand directions for drawing a sailboat. (Use at least five sentences.) Draw examples of each step that you took to draw the sailboat.

Ensemble Assemble

Describe your favorite summer outfit in at least five sentences. If you don't have a favorite outfit, describe one that you would like to own. Then draw a picture of this outfit.

Warm And Cool Sailboats

Warm colors include shades of red and yellow. Cool colors include shades of blue and green. Draw two different pictures of a sailboat. Color one of the sailboats in warm colors, and the other picture in cool colors. Which picture do you like better? What feelings and emotions do warm colors evoke? What feelings and emotions do cool colors evoke?

Name